THE PEOPLE ON MY STREET

D1532358

By Judy Kentor Schmauss
Illustrated by Barry Ablett

BARRON'S

Table of Contents

Illustrations on pages 21–23 created by Carol Stutz

All inquiries should be addressed to:
Barron's Educational Series, Inc.
250 Wireless Boulevard
Hauppauge, New York 11788
www.barronseduc.com

Library of Congress Catalog Card No.: 2005054861

ISBN-13: 978-0-7641-3294-0
ISBN-10: 0-7641-3294-6

Library of Congress Cataloging-in-Publication Data
Schmauss, Judy Kentor.
    The people on my street / Judy Kentor Schmauss.
     p. cm. – (Reader's clubhouse)
    Summary: A young boy describes the occupations of the people living on his
neighborhood including the dentist, the teacher, the handyman, and the policeman.
    ISBN-13: 978-0-7641-3294-0
    ISBN-10: 0-7641-3294-6
    (1. Neighborhood—Fiction. 2. Occupations—Fiction.) I. Title. II. Series.

PZ7.S34736Pe 2006
(E)—dc22

                                          2005054861

PRINTED IN CHINA
9 8 7 6 5 4 3 2

Dear Parent and Educator,

Welcome to the Barron's Reader's Clubhouse, a series of books that provide a phonics approach to reading.

Phonics is the relationship between letters and sounds. It is a system that teaches children that letters have specific sounds. Level 1 books introduce the short-vowel sounds. Level 2 books progress to the long-vowel sounds. This progression matches how phonics is taught in many classrooms.

The People on My Street introduces the long "e" sound. Simple words with this long-vowel sound are called **decodable words.** The child knows how to sound out these words because he or she has learned the sound they include. This story also contains **high-frequency words.** These are common, everyday words that the child learns to read by sight. High-frequency words help ensure fluency and comprehension. **Challenging words** go a little beyond the reading level. The child will identify these words with help from the illustration on the page. All words are listed by their category on page 24.

Here are some coaching and prompting statements you can use to help a young reader read *The People on My Street:*

- **On page 4, "street" is a decodable word. Point to the word and say:**

  Read this word. How did you know the word? What sounds did it make?

  Note: There are many opportunities to repeat the above instruction throughout the book.

- **On page 10, "Dr." is a challenging word. Point to the word and say:**

  Read this word. Look at the beginning sound. How did you know the word? Did you look at the picture? How did it help?

You'll find more coaching ideas on the Reader's Clubhouse Web site: *www.barronsclubhouse.com.* Reader's Clubhouse is designed to teach and reinforce reading skills in a fun way. We hope you enjoy helping children discover their love of reading!

Sincerely,

Nancy Harris

Nancy Harris
Reading Consultant

This is my street.
This is where I eat and sleep.

Come meet the people on
my street.

This is Zeke.

We get meat, beans, and cheese from Zeke.

This is Neal.

Neal likes to plant seeds and
pull up weeds.

This is Dr. Deke.

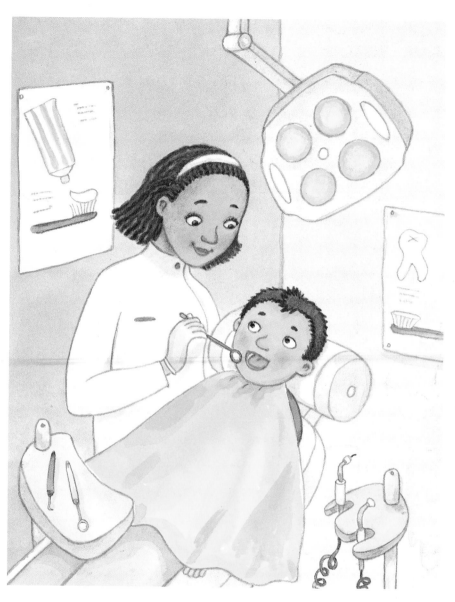

This week she will clean
my teeth.

This is Eve.

She can teach me to read.

This is Steve.

Steve can fix our screen.

This is Reece.

She feeds the geese at
the pond.

This is Pete.
He helps all the people on
our street.

I like our street!

Fun Facts About
Communities

- There are many types of communities. An anthill is an example of an animal community. A beehive is another example of an animal community.

- The insects in these communities all have specific jobs, just like the people in your community!

- Children are a big part of a community. You can help others in your community by picking up garbage, walking a neighbor's dog, or teaching someone how to read.

- In the 1960s, many communities began celebrating Earth Day to help save our environment. Today, many people hold recycling drives on Earth Day.

- All towns and cities are a little different from each other. Does the map of this community look like yours?

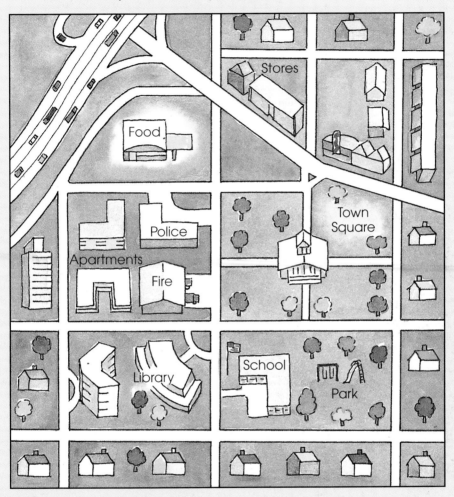

Coffee Can Bank

An Earth Day recycling drive is a great way to help keep your community clean. But you don't have to wait for Earth Day to recycle. Every day, you can find ways of recycling plastic, metal, and paper objects by making them into other useful things.

You will need:
- empty can with a plastic lid
- craft knife
- construction paper
- safety scissors
- glue
- rubber bands
- crayons, markers, stickers, feathers, glitter

1. Have an adult use the craft knife to make a slit in the middle of the plastic lid. It should be large enough to fit any coin.

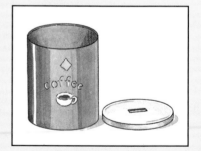

2. Cut a rectangle out of the paper that will wrap around the can.

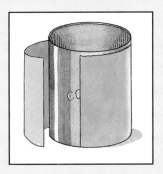

3. Lay the sheet of paper on a flat surface. Decorate it with crayons, markers, stickers, feathers, and glitter.

4. Glue the paper to the can. Secure the paper with rubber bands until the glue is dry.

Word List

Challenging Words	Dr.		
Long E Decodable Words	beans cheese clean Deke Eve feeds geese meat meet	Neal people Pete read Reece screen seeds sleep Steve	street teach teeth we weeds week Zeke
High-Frequency Words	all and at can come eat from get he helps I is like	likes me my on our she the this to up where	